Presidential Crisis Decisions

Presidential Crisis Decisions

Quick Insights Into How U.S. Leaders Managed Moments of National Peril

By

Robert Bosworth

Published by Prodigy Press
Printed in the United States of America.

For permissions or inquiries, contact:
prodigypress77@gmail.com

To the men and women who dedicate their lives to serving the nation, often behind the scenes, and to every leader who has carried the weight of decision-making under the gravest of circumstances.

May we continue to learn from the past and strive for a better future.

CONTENTS

Prologue: Inside the Nerve Center of Power

The White House Situation Room is more than just a room—it's the heartbeat of American decision-making in moments of profound consequence. Hidden beneath the West Wing, this space has borne witness to history as it unfolded in real time. From the quiet tension of Cold War standoffs to the chaos of terrorist attacks and the sobering reality of domestic unrest, the Situation Room stands as a silent participant in events that shape the nation and the world.

This book offers a rare glimpse into that sacred space, peeling back the layers of secrecy to reveal the weight of the decisions made within its walls. It is a story of leaders confronted with impossible choices, grappling with limited information and high stakes. Each chapter draws readers into moments where the clock ticked louder, the air grew heavier, and the outcome was far from certain.

The story begins with the vision of President John F. Kennedy, whose experience with the Bay of Pigs failure inspired the creation of this room—a place where future presidents could confront crises with the best tools and minds at their disposal. From that point forward, the Situation Room has been a crucible for crisis management, evolving alongside the complexities of global politics and modern warfare.

This book does not seek to merely recount history; it aims to immerse readers in the urgency and emotion of these defining moments. How did leadership react when American soil was attacked on **9/11?** What calculations went into the decision to send a team of Navy SEALs into Pakistan on a mission fraught with risk? And what role did this room play during the Capitol riots, a moment of reckoning for American democracy?

Each chapter takes you closer to understanding the humanity behind the headlines—the doubt, courage, and resilience of those tasked with steering the ship of state through turbulent waters. It is a journey into the psychology of leadership, the nuances of collaboration under pressure, and the unrelenting pursuit of solutions in the face of adversity.

As we explore the pivotal events and the evolution of this iconic room, one thing becomes clear: the Situation Room is not merely a setting for decisions; it is a testament to the enduring strength and fragility of democracy. It reminds us that leadership is not about avoiding crises but confronting them head-on, with resolve and an unwavering commitment to the greater good. Welcome to the Situation Room—a place where history is made, one decision at a time.

Introduction

The White House Situation Room holds a unique and vital place in the heart of American history, representing a space where the most pivotal decisions in U.S. history have been made. As the country's primary crisis management hub, it serves as the epicenter for presidential decision-making during national emergencies, security threats, and high-stakes situations. This room, often shrouded in secrecy and behind-the-scenes deliberations, is where America's most consequential moments are often determined in real-time.

The Situation Room's significance is rooted in its role as the command center for the President of the United States and the key members of their national security team. From the moment it was created by President *John F. Kennedy* in the early 1960s, this room became integral to the

U.S. government's response to crises, both domestic and international. The Situation Room allows for the rapid exchange of intelligence, ensuring the President is fully briefed on every potential threat to the nation. The room's features—secure communications systems, classified information, and advanced technology—are specifically designed to enable quick, informed, and precise decision-making. Through these capabilities, presidents have been able to address crises ranging from military conflicts to natural disasters, each decision often carrying immense consequences.

Kennedy's creation of the Situation Room marked a transformative moment in how the U.S. approached national security. Prior to its establishment, communication within the White House was often disjointed, and decisions were made without a centralized space for coordinating national defense. The Cuban Missile Crisis of 1962 underscored the need for an organized structure, with the situation room becoming the go-to place for real-time updates and strategic discussions during the tense standoff with the Soviet Union. It was in this room where Kennedy and his advisers worked tirelessly to prevent an all-out nuclear war, relying on timely intelligence and constant communication with military leaders.

Over the years, the Situation Room has become more than just a place for briefings—it is a vital component of presidential decision-making during global crises. Successive administrations have continued to use it for everything from military operations to diplomatic negotiations. Its technology and physical infrastructure have evolved, with advancements allowing for more secure and faster communication between the President, military leaders, and intelligence agencies. Today, the Situation Room's secure network allows the President and their team to assess global threats instantaneously, facilitating coordinated responses to emerging dangers.

This book offers an unprecedented look inside the White House Situation Room, giving readers access to some of the most critical moments in U.S. history. Through detailed accounts of past crises, the book will take readers through the tense, often nerve-wracking decisions that shaped the course of nations and lives. We'll explore key moments where U.S. Presidents have faced life-or-death situations, where the stakes were so high that the fate of the nation, and even the world, rested on the shoulders of those in the room. Each chapter will uncover the decisions, actions, and consequences of these pivotal moments—decisions that not only changed the direction of American history but had far-reaching impacts on global geopolitics.

For instance, the Cuban Missile Crisis stands as one of the most defining moments in the history of the Situation Room. As the Soviet Union placed nuclear missiles in Cuba, the room became the crucible for the Kennedy administration's decisions that would prevent a nuclear disaster. With military leaders urging a more aggressive response, it was ultimately Kennedy's calm leadership and reliance on the Situation Room's intelligence that led to a peaceful resolution. The book will examine this crisis closely, shedding light on the dynamics of Kennedy's decision-making process and how the

Situation Room facilitated a response that avoided catastrophe.

Another unforgettable crisis that will be explored in this book is ***the raid to capture and kill Osama bin Laden in 2011.*** President Obama's decision to authorize the operation came after months of painstaking intelligence gathering. The Situation Room served as the nerve center during the raid, with real-time communication and surveillance updates coming directly to the President. The book will provide readers with an inside look at the pressure faced by Obama and his advisers, highlighting the high stakes of the operation and the split-second decisions that would determine its success or failure. This mission represents one of the most remarkable moments in modern U.S. history and underscores the extraordinary importance of the Situation Room in managing such complex military operations.

Throughout this book, we will also explore lesser-known yet equally significant moments, such as the tense moments during the 9/11 attacks. The Situation Room was instrumental in coordinating the U.S. government's response, where President George W. Bush and his team had to make swift decisions in the face of uncertainty and chaos. From military responses to intelligence operations, the Situation Room was the central location for all aspects of the U.S. government's reaction to the most devastating attack on American soil in modern history.

In examining these events, the book aims to take readers behind closed doors into the room where history is made. We'll learn not just about the decisions, but also about the people who made them—those who were part of the tense, high-pressure environment of the Situation Room. From the military officers and intelligence experts to the political advisers and the President himself, we will gain insights into how the collaboration between these individuals led to life-altering outcomes. The book will also reflect on the evolution of this space over time, exploring how advancements in technology and shifts in global geopolitics have shaped the role of the Situation Room in modern-day crisis management.

As readers turn the pages of this book, they'll witness moments of history from a vantage point that has long been kept secret. This isn't just a recounting of historical events; it's an exploration of the critical decisions that have shaped the United States and the world. Through these accounts, readers will better understand the immense responsibility carried by the President and their advisers and the complexities involved in making decisions that affect millions of lives. The Situation Room is not merely a room; it is the heart of American crisis management—a place where the course of history can change in an instant.

The impact of the decisions made in this room is profound. They reverberate through the political landscape, influencing not just national policy but the lives of people across the globe. Through this book, we'll learn that while the Situation Room may be a physical space, its impact stretches far beyond the walls of the White House. The choices made there, and the consequences of those choices, are what define the American presidency and, at times, the fate of nations. This is a story of leadership under pressure, of moments when decisions cannot afford to be wrong. It is a story of how the most powerful nation in the world responds to the greatest challenges it faces—inside the Situation Room.

CHAPTER 1

The Birth of the Situation Room

The White House Situation Room is a symbol of American leadership during times of crisis, but its creation was far from inevitable. It emerged from a specific historical context marked by failure, urgency, and the need for reform. The pivotal event that led to the establishment of the Situation Room was the Bay of Pigs invasion of 1961, a failed military operation that deeply affected President John F. Kennedy's leadership and his approach to managing crises.

The Bay of Pigs was a disastrous attempt to overthrow the Cuban government led by Fidel Castro, orchestrated by the CIA and supported by a group of Cuban exiles. The mission, which began on April 17, 1961, quickly collapsed, and the failure embarrassed the Kennedy administration. The operation's failure not only humiliated the U.S. but also jeopardized the country's standing in the Cold War. The event exposed weaknesses in communication, decision-making, and crisis management, which prompted Kennedy to re-evaluate how the U.S. government responded to national security threats.

The Bay of Pigs disaster demonstrated the need for a more effective and organized way to manage crises, especially during high-stakes situations where quick decisions were essential. In the aftermath, Kennedy and his advisers recognized that they needed a centralized, secure location where they could receive real-time intelligence, coordinate military and diplomatic responses, and consult with their key advisors. This insight led to the establishment of the White House Situation Room.

Kennedy's leadership during this time was a defining factor in the room's creation. He recognized that past crises had revealed the flaws in the U.S. government's ability to act decisively. Prior to the creation of the Situation Room, presidents and their teams had to rely on separate communication channels, which could be slow and uncoordinated. The Bay of Pigs, in particular, showed the importance of having immediate access to accurate intelligence, expert advice, and secure communication, all of which could enable a president to make decisions more effectively.

Kennedy's vision was clear: he wanted a place where national security and military experts could collaborate seamlessly with the president, particularly in moments when every minute counted. He tasked his team with creating a secure, accessible, and technologically advanced space that would facilitate fast decision-making during international and domestic crises. The room would be equipped with secure communications and surveillance capabilities, ensuring that the President would have access to the most up-to-date information, no matter the time or location.

The initial design of the Situation Room reflected Kennedy's understanding of the need for comprehensive and streamlined operations. Situated deep within the White House complex, it was strategically positioned to provide privacy and security for the president and his team. The room was outfitted with state-of-the-art communication equipment, including secure telephones, radio lines, and direct access to military and intelligence channels. The room was also designed to be staffed around the clock, ensuring that there would always be a team ready to respond to a crisis, even in the middle of the night.

As Kennedy's leadership evolved, so too did the purpose and significance of the Situation Room. The Cuban Missile Crisis, which occurred just over a year later, became the first major test for the newly formed space. During this pivotal 13-day standoff in October 1962, Kennedy and his team were faced with the threat of nuclear war as Soviet missiles were discovered in Cuba. The Situation Room became the central hub for real-time updates and discussions, as Kennedy worked with his advisers to carefully consider the consequences of military action versus diplomatic negotiation.

The Cuban Missile Crisis showed the world how effective crisis management could be with the right tools and information at hand. It was inside the Situation Room that Kennedy and his advisers worked tirelessly, using intelligence reports, military input, and international analysis to make decisions that ultimately avoided catastrophic conflict. The room's ability to support a coordinated response was instrumental in preventing a full-scale war and highlighted the importance of centralized communication in managing national security threats.

The experience of the Cuban Missile Crisis also demonstrated the room's adaptability. While it had been designed primarily to manage crises like the Bay of Pigs invasion, it quickly became clear that the Situation Room needed to evolve in response to the changing landscape of international politics and military technology. The Cold War, with its increasing nuclear threat and complex geopolitical tensions, required an ever-more sophisticated operation to meet the challenges of the day. In response, the Situation Room's role expanded beyond military operations to include diplomatic crises, covert operations, and intelligence gathering.

The Bay of Pigs and the Cuban Missile Crisis set the tone for the Situation Room's future. The lessons learned from these events shaped not only Kennedy's presidency but also those of his successors. The Situation Room became an indispensable tool for every subsequent president, especially as Cold War tensions escalated. Throughout the 1960s and 1970s, the U.S. faced numerous crises—from the Vietnam War to the Arab-Israeli conflicts—all of which were managed, at least in part, from the Situation Room.

As time went on, the Situation Room continued to evolve with new technological advances and the changing nature of warfare. The rise of satellite technology, the development of real-time communications, and the need for rapid decision-making in the face of terrorism and nuclear proliferation made the Situation Room an ever-more crucial asset for the presidency. Its role would only grow more important in the years that followed, as U.S. presidents faced an increasing range of global threats.

What began under President Kennedy as a response to a specific crisis became, over the years, a permanent and vital feature of the White House. Its role in managing national security, military operations, and diplomatic responses has continued to be a cornerstone of presidential leadership. The Situation Room stands as a testament to the enduring need for coordination, communication, and quick decision-making during times of crisis, as well as to Kennedy's foresight in understanding the importance of these qualities for the future of American security.

As the book progresses, we will explore how the room's creation shaped the course of history and how its operations have influenced key moments in U.S. history, from the Cold War to the modern-day War on Terror. But first, it's essential to understand that the origins of the Situation Room lay in one man's leadership and his commitment to ensuring that the President of the United States would have the tools necessary to make life-and-death decisions during the most dangerous of times. Kennedy's creation of the Situation Room changed the way presidents would respond to crises, and it continues to shape the way the U.S. handles national security to this day.

CHAPTER 2

The Kennedy and Reagan Shootings: Crisis Under Fire

On the afternoon of November 22, 1963, the United States found itself thrust into a crisis that would alter the course of history. President John F. Kennedy, beloved by millions, was shot and killed while riding in a motorcade in Dallas, Texas. Less than 20 years later, in March 1981, President Ronald Reagan faced an assassination attempt of his own. Both moments, though separated by decades, revealed the extraordinary pressures of crisis management and underscored the critical role of the White House Situation Room in orchestrating immediate responses to national emergencies.

When the news of Kennedy's shooting broke, the country was gripped with disbelief. Kennedy had been struck by bullets fired from a nearby Texas school book depot. As the nation watched in horror, the president was rushed to Parkland

Memorial Hospital in Dallas, but tragically, he did not survive. Within moments of the attack, the Situation Room sprang to life, coordinating efforts to ensure a swift and effective response.

Key figures in the Situation Room, including National Security Advisor McGeorge Bundy, Secretary of Defense Robert McNamara, and FBI Director J. Edgar Hoover, were immediately alerted to the unfolding tragedy. The room became the central hub for communication between the White House, law enforcement agencies, and the military. Kennedy's death was not just a national tragedy; it was a security crisis that demanded a coordinated response to preserve the continuity of government and the safety of the nation.

One of the first critical decisions in the Situation Room was the verification of President Kennedy's condition and the subsequent determination that Vice President Lyndon B. Johnson would assume the presidency. This was a moment of extraordinary importance, and the Situation Room ensured that Johnson was quickly moved to Air Force One for a safe departure. The location of Johnson's swearing-in ceremony, which took place on the plane on the tarmac at Dallas Love Field, was chosen with careful consideration. The Situation Room was fully involved in determining the logistical details of the transfer of power, which took place swiftly and seamlessly despite the chaos of the day.

A major concern during this crisis was national security, particularly the fear of a broader conspiracy or a potential follow-up attack. In those tense moments, military readiness and intelligence gathering became paramount. McNamara and other top advisers in the Situation Room were charged with ensuring that the military stood at a heightened alert level. The Cold War had created a climate of suspicion, and Kennedy's assassination raised fears that it might be tied to a larger plot, possibly even involving foreign enemies. The Situation Room handled communications with military leaders, readying them for possible responses, even though no immediate action was required.

The assassination of President Kennedy was a turning point in American political history, one that redefined national security protocols. It led to an expansion of security measures, including more rigorous procedures for protecting the president and other top officials. The Kennedy assassination also revealed the need for a more coordinated and centralized command center to deal with the extraordinary pressures of such events. In the wake of Kennedy's death, the White House Situation Room gained a new sense of purpose and prominence, playing an even larger role in overseeing the country's response to national emergencies.

Fast forward to March 30, 1981, and President Ronald Reagan faced an assassination attempt of his own. Reagan, having just delivered a speech outside the Washington Hilton Hotel, was shot by John Hinckley Jr., a troubled individual who believed that the attack would impress actress Jodie Foster. The moment was chilling in its own right, as Reagan was struck by a bullet that punctured his lung and came dangerously close to his heart. Despite his serious injuries, Reagan remained conscious, maintaining his composure and even joking with his doctors as he was rushed to the hospital.

Once again, the White House Situation Room became the focal point of the response. This time, however, there were new security protocols in place, shaped in part by the lessons learned from Kennedy's assassination. Reagan's shooting was handled with incredible speed and precision, though the uncertainty surrounding his condition added to the tension of the moment. The Situation Room coordinated with the White House staff, the Secret Service, and the medical team, ensuring that every available resource was directed toward stabilizing the president's health.

Immediately following the shooting, Reagan's Chief of Staff, James Baker, along with National Security Advisor Richard Allen, took charge of the situation. They had to make swift decisions regarding Reagan's health and security, ensuring that both the president and the country were safe. The White House's contingency plans, developed in the years following the Kennedy assassination, were put into action, including transferring power temporarily to Vice President George H.W. Bush as Reagan underwent surgery. The Situation Room facilitated direct communication between key players in the administration, military leaders, and medical personnel, ensuring that there was no lapse in leadership during this critical time.

One of the key decisions made in the Situation Room during the Reagan shooting was the activation of emergency protocols designed to ensure national security. Like Kennedy's shooting, there was immediate concern about whether the attack was part of a larger conspiracy. Intelligence reports were closely monitored, and the military was placed on heightened alert. The concern wasn't just for Reagan's safety but also for the integrity of the U.S. government. The Situation Room was responsible for ensuring that the nation's leadership remained intact while the president was incapacitated.

Both the Kennedy and Reagan shootings tested the United States' ability to respond to crises at the highest levels. The aftermath of these events led to a dramatic shift in national security measures. Kennedy's assassination directly contributed to the evolution of the Situation Room, which would later handle emergencies like the 9/11 attacks and the 2008 financial crisis. The experiences of those fateful days shaped a generation of crisis management protocols that prioritized speed, communication, and the preservation of American leadership in times of peril.

In the years that followed the Reagan shooting, the lessons learned were evident in the country's preparedness for crises. Security measures for presidents were dramatically improved, and the Situation Room's role became even more crucial as the U.S. faced new and unpredictable threats, both at home and abroad.

Ultimately, these two crises—Kennedy's tragic death and Reagan's survival—illustrated the extraordinary pressures on the U.S. government when the life of a sitting president is on the line. Each event underscored the vital role of the Situation Room in coordinating rapid responses to national emergencies, ensuring continuity of government, and stabilizing the nation in times of peril. They remain defining moments in U.S. history, offering timeless lessons in leadership, decision-making, and the importance of preparation when confronting the unknown.

CHAPTER 3

Nixon's DEFCON III Alert: A National Security Crisis

In October 1973, President Richard Nixon found himself embroiled in multiple crises, both personal and political, which threatened the stability of his presidency. Amidst the fallout from the Watergate scandal, Nixon faced a different kind of emergency: an international military threat that required a swift and decisive response. It was during this tense period, marked by heightened Cold War tensions and political turbulence, that Nixon raised the United States military's readiness to DEFCON III, the second-highest alert level, signaling a national security crisis. The events surrounding this decision would be pivotal not only for American military strategy but also in understanding the intersection of political, personal, and global pressures faced by a president under fire.

The crisis began with the outbreak of the Yom Kippur War on October 6, 1973, when Egypt and Syria launched a surprise attack on Israel. The U.S., a staunch ally of Israel, found itself at the center of a potential Cold War confrontation. The Soviet Union, which supported the Arab nations, warned the U.S. not to intervene, and tensions quickly escalated between the superpowers. As the Soviet Union began sending military aid to the Arab states, the risk of direct confrontation between the two nuclear-armed giants grew. In this high-stakes atmosphere, Nixon was confronted with an urgent decision: how to support Israel without triggering a broader war with the Soviets.

On the same day that war broke out in the Middle East, Nixon faced political instability at home. The Watergate scandal had reached a boiling point, with the ongoing investigation threatening to unravel his presidency. His approval ratings were plummeting, and his administration was under intense scrutiny. But despite the political chaos surrounding him, Nixon's focus shifted to the international crisis, and the urgency of the situation in the Middle East demanded his immediate attention.

In response to the rapidly escalating conflict, Nixon ordered a military alert to DEFCON III on October 24, 1973. This alert level, only one step away from full-scale nuclear readiness, marked the first time since the Cuban Missile Crisis that the U.S. military had raised its alert to this level. The move sent shockwaves through the Situation Room, where military officials, including Secretary of Defense James Schlesinger and National Security Advisor Henry Kissinger, convened to assess the situation and determine the next course of action.

The tension in the Situation Room was palpable. The decision to raise the DEFCON level was not taken lightly, as it carried significant ramifications. Raising the alert level was an indication that the U.S. was prepared to engage in military action if necessary. For Nixon, this decision had the dual purpose of demonstrating American resolve in protecting its allies and sending a clear message to the Soviet Union that the U.S. would not back down. However, the political pressures Nixon was under at home created an environment where even routine decisions became clouded with additional considerations.

At the time, Nixon was also struggling with his personal demons, including his ongoing battle with alcoholism. While his drinking had been a well-guarded secret throughout much of his political career, it was widely understood by his closest advisers that Nixon's judgment was sometimes impaired by alcohol. This aspect of his leadership style was crucial to understanding the gravity of the situation in the Situation Room. Nixon's inner circle, including Kissinger and Chief of Staff Alexander Haig, had to make crucial decisions while managing not only the military response but also the complex and unpredictable nature of Nixon's mood and temperament.

This mix of personal factors and national security concerns created a volatile atmosphere in which decisions were made, often in a state of uncertainty. Nixon's alcoholism played a role in his decision-making during the crisis, as he sometimes appeared detached and distracted during critical moments. Kissinger, in particular, was forced to step in on several occasions to help guide the president's actions. The dynamics within the Situation Room were complicated by these personal issues, with the urgency of the military threat in the Middle East requiring quick decisions that were not always easy to make in the midst of such political and personal turmoil.

In response to the DEFCON III alert, military commanders on the ground were placed on high alert, and strategic decisions were made to prepare for potential escalation. The U.S. increased its military presence in the Mediterranean and the Middle East, and diplomatic channels with the Soviet Union were opened in an attempt to de-escalate tensions. The situation remained tense for several weeks, but Nixon's decision to raise the alert level and support Israel with military aid proved to be a pivotal moment in the U.S. response to the Yom Kippur War.

The impact of Nixon's DEFCON III alert was far-reaching. While the situation in the Middle East eventually de-escalated, the decision to raise the military alert signaled to both the Soviet Union and the world that the U.S. was prepared to defend its interests and allies at all costs. The crisis also had long-lasting effects on American military strategy. The alert emphasized the need for clear communication and quick decision-making during international crises. The lessons learned from this event influenced future presidential responses to military threats, particularly during the height of the Cold War.

Moreover, the crisis highlighted the important role of the Situation Room in managing not only military threats but also the political and personal dynamics of the president's leadership. The tensions within the room—between military officials, diplomats, and the president's inner circle—revealed the complex and often delicate balance of decision-making under extreme pressure. The personal challenges Nixon faced only added to the already fraught nature of the situation, underscoring the importance of having a strong and decisive leadership team to handle moments of crisis.

In the years following the Yom Kippur War, the DEFCON III alert became a significant moment in U.S. military history. The incident also contributed to the evolution of the Situation Room, which continued to serve as the central command center for crisis management. The lessons learned from this crisis would resonate through subsequent administrations, where the capacity to respond quickly and decisively to international threats became ever more critical.

In retrospect, the DEFCON III alert during Nixon's presidency serves as a reminder of the difficult decisions faced by U.S. leaders in moments of national security crisis. Nixon's political and personal struggles complicated an already tense situation, but in the end, the country emerged from the crisis without direct military confrontation. The event was a testament to the power of the White House Situation Room in managing high-stakes moments, and the enduring impact of Nixon's decision continues to influence U.S. military strategy today.

CHAPTER 4

Carter and the Hostage Rescue: A Gamble in Crisis

The Iran Hostage Crisis of 1979-1981 remains one of the most defining moments of President Jimmy Carter's tenure, encapsulating the complexities of diplomacy, military operations, and high-stakes decision-making in times of national distress. The crisis began on November 4, 1979, when 52 American diplomats and citizens were taken hostage by Iranian militants who stormed the U.S. Embassy in Tehran. For the next 444 days, the hostages would endure unimaginable conditions, while President Carter's administration grappled with one of the most challenging foreign policy crises in American history. The Situation Room played a pivotal role in coordinating the U.S. response, which included both traditional military operations and unorthodox methods, including consulting psychics for guidance.

From the outset, the Iran Hostage Crisis posed an unprecedented test of leadership. Carter's first instinct was to pursue diplomatic solutions, attempting to resolve the situation through negotiations with the Iranian government. However, the militants' demands were vague and their stance inflexible. As days turned to weeks, it became clear that diplomacy alone would not bring the hostages home. Faced with this grim reality, Carter and his national security team turned to military options, hoping that a rescue mission could extract the hostages from their captors.

The Situation Room became the nerve center for decision-making throughout this period. Led by Carter and his closest advisers, the room was where the president, military commanders, intelligence officers, and diplomats worked to assess the evolving situation. Every action had to be carefully weighed for its potential to escalate the crisis, and the pressure was immense. Military operations were considered, but the logistical and political challenges of launching a rescue mission were daunting.

One of the most infamous episodes in this chapter of U.S. history was the ill-fated rescue mission known as Operation Eagle Claw. The operation, planned to rescue the hostages by storming the U.S. Embassy compound in Tehran, involved a series of bold and daring military maneuvers. The plan called for special forces teams to infiltrate Iran, supported by a complex array of airlift and logistics. The mission, however, faced numerous obstacles from the start. Poor planning, logistical miscalculations, and unforeseen technical failures plagued the operation. A critical blow occurred when a helicopter, essential for the mission's success, crashed in the Iranian desert. The failure of the mission, with American lives at stake, was a major setback for Carter and his administration.

This disastrous turn of events led to growing frustration in the Situation Room. With Operation Eagle Claw failing, Carter's team turned to other unconventional methods to bring the hostages home. Among the more extraordinary proposals was the suggestion to consult psychic advisers, who would supposedly offer insights or guidance on the rescue operation. This idea, often viewed with skepticism, seemed to be a sign of the desperation that gripped the administration. In the charged atmosphere of the Situation Room, the use of psychics became an emblem of how far Carter was willing to go, within reason, to find a solution to the crisis.

The decision to use psychics was influenced by Carter's personal interest in alternative approaches. It was reported that Carter had previously been interested in holistic and unconventional solutions to problems, and during the hostage crisis, these inclinations were brought to the fore. While some of the more rational voices in the room dismissed the idea as a far-fetched last resort, Carter and his team explored every option available. The psychic advisers were tasked with offering predictions or guidance on where the hostages were held and whether the rescue mission had a reasonable chance of success. It remains unclear whether the psychics had any direct impact on the outcome, but the decision to explore this avenue underlined the extreme pressure felt by Carter and his team.

Beyond the psychics, the Situation Room also remained the command center for planning future military operations. In response to the failed rescue attempt, the U.S. focused more intently on diplomatic strategies, using international pressure to push Iran into negotiations. Meanwhile, the U.S. military maintained a state of readiness in the Persian Gulf, prepared to intervene if necessary. The Carter administration's policy was one of a multifaceted approach, where diplomacy, military options, and unconventional strategies were blended together in an effort to resolve the crisis.

While the failed mission and reliance on unconventional methods cast a shadow over Carter's handling of the crisis, it is important to consider the broader context of the Situation Room's role. The room itself was a central hub of national security decision-making, coordinating responses to rapidly shifting events in the volatile Middle East. Every decision made within the Situation Room had significant implications, both for the lives of the hostages and for the U.S.'s reputation abroad. Carter's team was under intense scrutiny, not only from the American public but also from the rest of the world. The failure to free the hostages, combined with the escalating political costs of the crisis, led to Carter's loss of re-election in 1980.

Despite the failed mission and the unconventional measures considered, the crisis ultimately concluded on January 20, 1981, when the hostages were released shortly after Ronald Reagan was inaugurated as president. The release was likely influenced by the negotiations brokered by Algeria, but the timing of the release also symbolized the end of the Carter presidency. The ordeal was a key factor in Carter's inability to secure a second term, as Americans were deeply frustrated with the ongoing crisis and the perceived inability of the U.S. government to resolve it.

The Iran Hostage Crisis, and the way it was handled in the Situation Room, left a lasting legacy on U.S. foreign policy. The experience underscored the limitations of military intervention in a complex political environment and highlighted the dangers of over-relying on unproven methods. For Carter, the crisis was an emotional and political setback, but it also shaped his future humanitarian efforts. The crisis's resolution, though bittersweet, reinforced the importance of diplomatic engagement, military readiness, and the value of a broad array of strategies when addressing high-stakes international crises.

Looking back, the Iran Hostage Crisis serves as a powerful reminder of the high cost of national security decisions and the weight of leadership during times of extreme crisis. The Situation Room was at the center of these decisions, a place where American lives and international relations were at stake, and where every choice had the potential to reverberate far beyond the confines of the room itself. For President Carter, the hostage crisis was an ordeal that would forever shape his presidency, and the lessons learned in the Situation Room during that time continue to resonate in the way U.S. presidents approach crisis management today.

CHAPTER 5

9/11: The Crisis that Defined a Nation

The morning of September 11, 2001, began like any other. Yet, within the span of a few hours, it became one of the darkest chapters in American history. Four commercial airplanes were hijacked by terrorists from al-Qaeda, two of which crashed into the Twin Towers of the World Trade Center in New York City, while another struck the Pentagon in Arlington, Virginia. The fourth plane, United Airlines Flight 93, crashed into a field in Pennsylvania after passengers fought the hijackers. The attacks killed nearly 3,000 people and changed the course of history.

The White House Situation Room, which had become the nerve center for national security decisions, was thrust into the heart of this crisis. President George W. Bush, his senior advisors, and military and intelligence personnel gathered in this secure location to respond to the most devastating attack on U.S. soil in modern history. The decisions made in those early moments would define the nation's response and shape the trajectory of U.S. foreign and domestic policy for years to come.

The Immediate Chaos

It was just after 8:46 a.m. when American Airlines Flight 11 struck the North Tower of the World Trade Center. As the nation watched in horror, it became clear that the United States was under attack. At the time, President Bush was in a classroom in Sarasota, Florida, meeting with a group of schoolchildren. The President's Chief of Staff, Andrew Card, whispered in his ear that a second plane had struck the South Tower, confirming the worst fears—this was no accident.

At that moment, Bush was quickly taken to Air Force One for security reasons, but back in Washington, the Situation Room came alive. The room, a high-tech, classified area deep within the White House, was filled with advisors, military officers, intelligence experts, and White House staff. They began coordinating the government's response, even as the scope of the disaster was still unclear.

Key members of the team included Vice President Dick Cheney, National Security Advisor Condoleezza Rice, and the President's Chief of Staff Andrew Card. Among them was General Richard Myers, who was named acting Chairman of the Joint Chiefs of Staff as General Hugh Shelton was out of town. They were faced with a rapidly evolving situation, and their decisions were critical in determining how the nation would respond.

The Situation Room Comes to Life

As the news of the attacks unfolded, the Situation Room became the focal point for gathering and analyzing information. Real-time intelligence reports poured in from the FBI, CIA, and National Security Agency, detailing the status of the hijacked planes, the extent of the destruction, and potential threats still on the horizon. At the same time, military assets were being mobilized to secure the skies and respond to any further attacks. Fighter jets were scrambled, and the Federal Aviation Administration (FAA) grounded all planes in U.S. airspace.

One of the first critical decisions made was to establish a no-fly zone. By 9:30 a.m., all civilian aircraft were ordered to land, and military jets were patrolling the skies, prepared to intercept any planes that were still unaccounted for. As the news came in about the Pentagon being hit, the situation escalated from a terrorist attack to a full-blown national security crisis.

Inside the Situation Room, President Bush was briefed on the latest developments, including the fact that a third plane had struck the Pentagon. The President's immediate priority was to ensure the safety of the nation's leaders and military personnel. As the President was flown back to Washington, Vice President Cheney remained in the White House bunker, continuing to lead the government's response from the Situation Room.

It was in these early hours that a series of important decisions had to be made. The U.S. military moved swiftly to secure critical infrastructure, including key government buildings, while intelligence agencies worked to identify the perpetrators behind the attacks. The coordination of federal agencies was crucial, and the Situation Room became the command hub for these efforts.

Key Decisions in the Moment

One of the most pivotal decisions made in the Situation Room was the determination of the nature of the attacks. Intelligence quickly suggested that this was not a random act of terrorism, but a well-coordinated assault planned by al-Qaeda. President Bush authorized the use of military force to respond to the attacks, though initially, the scope and nature of that response were unclear. The President's options ranged from targeted airstrikes against terrorist training camps to launching full-scale military action against the Taliban regime in Afghanistan, which had been harboring al-Qaeda leader Osama bin Laden.

Another decision that was debated heavily in the Situation Room was whether to take immediate military action or to wait for more information.

The urgency of the situation was apparent, but there was a recognition that any military response had to be strategic. The decision to use military force in the war on terror was not taken lightly, and the consequences of such actions were weighed heavily in the Situation Room.

As the nation reeled from the shock of the attacks, the decision was made to continue gathering intelligence on the identities of the hijackers and to ensure that the country remained protected from further attacks. The actions taken in those first few hours of the crisis were critical in preventing additional casualties and ensuring that the U.S. military was prepared for anything that followed.

Lasting Impact on U.S. Policy

The immediate decisions made in the Situation Room on 9/11 would have profound and lasting effects on U.S. policy. The attacks led directly to the creation of the Department of Homeland Security (DHS) in 2002 and the passage of the USA PATRIOT Act, which expanded the government's surveillance and counterterrorism powers. National security policy shifted dramatically, with a focus on preemptive strikes against terrorists and regimes that supported terrorism.

The decision to invade Afghanistan in late 2001 was another key outcome of the 9/11 attacks. The Taliban's refusal to hand over bin Laden and dismantle al-Qaeda training camps led to a military campaign that aimed to remove the Taliban from power and cripple al-Qaeda. The U.S. military's response to the 9/11 attacks would set the stage for the broader War on Terror, which would stretch across two decades and involve numerous conflicts around the globe.

In addition to military and policy changes, the 9/11 attacks left a lasting impact on American society. Homeland security measures became more stringent, airports implemented tighter security protocols, and the threat of terrorism became a constant backdrop to daily life. The tragedy of 9/11 became a defining moment in the American psyche, shaping the nation's response to crises for years to come.

The 9/11 attacks presented the United States with an unprecedented challenge that demanded swift, decisive action. The Situation Room, as the center of national defense and coordination, played an essential role in guiding the government's response. Through real-time decision-making and coordinated efforts across various agencies, the U.S. leadership confronted the immediate threat and began formulating a long-term strategy to combat terrorism.

The legacy of 9/11 continues to shape U.S. foreign policy, national security strategy, and domestic law enforcement practices. The decisions made in those early hours not only determined the response to the attacks but also set the course for America's future engagement with global terrorism. For the individuals in the Situation Room, the weight of these decisions was immense, but they carried the responsibility of securing the future of the nation.

CHAPTER 6

The Bin Laden Raid: A High-Risk Mission

The mission to kill or capture Osama bin Laden, the mastermind behind the September 11 attacks, was one of the most significant operations in U.S. history. By the time President Barack Obama authorized the raid on May 1, 2011, bin Laden had eluded capture for nearly a decade. The events leading up to the raid were tense, filled with strategic deliberations, intelligence gathering, and an atmosphere of uncertainty. It was inside the White House Situation Room that some of the most crucial decisions were made that would ultimately result in the end of one of the most notorious figures in modern terrorism.

The Build-Up: Years of Intelligence Gathering

The hunt for Osama bin Laden began immediately after the 9/11 attacks, but by 2011, despite years of searching, there had been little concrete evidence regarding his whereabouts. The breakthrough came in 2010 when CIA analysts, using a combination of intelligence from detainees, intercepted communications, and a high-value courier named Abu Ahmed al-Kuwaiti, began piecing together clues that led them to a compound in Abbottabad, Pakistan, where they believed bin Laden was hiding. The compound was located just a few hundred yards from a Pakistani military academy, raising both questions about the support he might have had within Pakistan and the diplomatic and political risks associated with the mission.

President Obama and his national security team were presented with a situation where the stakes were incredibly high. The intelligence was compelling, but there was still uncertainty about whether bin Laden was indeed in the compound. A strike against the compound could have severe diplomatic consequences, especially if Pakistan was unaware or opposed to the operation. The Situation Room was where these concerns were debated, with a clear sense of urgency to act while also weighing the potential risks involved.

The Decision-Making Process

In April 2011, after months of monitoring the compound, the intelligence community had gathered enough information to convince President Obama and his team that bin Laden was likely there. The President convened a meeting with his national security team to discuss the possible courses of action. The Situation Room became the focal point for these critical deliberations, as Obama and his advisors weighed the options.

There were two primary choices: a covert ground assault using Navy SEALs or an airstrike that would destroy the compound from the sky. The airstrike option was favored by some members of the team, as it would eliminate the risk of U.S. personnel on the ground, but it was ultimately rejected. The ground assault offered the best chance to capture bin Laden alive, which was a key objective, but it also carried significant risks.

Some members of the team, including Vice President Joe Biden, expressed concerns about the potential for failure and the consequences of a botched operation. The possibility of Pakistani resistance, or worse, the discovery of bin Laden's death before he could be captured, posed a dilemma for the U.S. administration. The SEAL mission would require a delicate and precise operation, with a high probability of a firefight. But ultimately, President Obama made the decisive call: the risk of not acting, and the opportunity to finally bring bin Laden to justice, outweighed the potential consequences.

The Role of Intelligence and Real-Time Decisions

As the clock ticked down toward the operation, the Situation Room was alive with activity. Intelligence reports were continuously filtered into the room, and the team worked feverishly to ensure that everything was in place. The CIA, FBI, and military worked together to confirm that the compound was indeed where bin Laden was believed to be, and to ensure that there were no surprises once the operation was launched.

The role of intelligence in the Bin Laden raid was unparalleled. The team relied on a variety of sources to verify the location and identify key details, such as the layout of the compound and the possible presence of other individuals. One of the most critical pieces of intelligence came from the testimony of a detainee, who had previously identified the courier as bin Laden's trusted aide. Over the course of several months, that intelligence was confirmed through various means, including satellite images and intercepted communications.

Additionally, the SEAL team had been trained specifically for this mission. They spent weeks preparing for every possible scenario, including the compound's layout, the potential for Pakistani military intervention, and the logistics of the helicopter insertions into the compound. Once the decision to move forward was made, every detail was meticulously executed, with constant updates from the field sent back to the Situation Room.

As the mission unfolded, the Situation Room remained the hub of communication and coordination. Real-time intelligence from the SEAL team was continuously sent back, and President Obama, Vice President Biden, Secretary of Defense Robert Gates, and other senior officials remained in constant communication. The mission was underway, but it was far from over.

The Raid: A Dangerous, High-Stakes Operation

The raid was conducted by Navy SEAL Team Six, a highly trained special operations unit, under the cover of night. The operation, known as Operation Neptune Spear, began with a helicopter assault that inserted the SEAL team into the compound. Once inside, the SEALs encountered fierce resistance from members of bin Laden's family and security personnel. The compound was fortified, and bin Laden was not immediately located, making the mission even more perilous.

The situation was tense. The SEALs had to breach multiple buildings to find bin Laden, all while ensuring their safety and the safety of those around them. After a thorough search of the compound, the SEALs found bin Laden in the third floor of the building. The decision was made to engage. Bin Laden was shot and killed, along with several others in the compound.

While the mission was a success, it was still unclear what would follow. The U.S. government had to ensure that the operation remained secret, particularly in the sensitive context of Pakistan's potential complicity. President Obama made the decision to keep the details of the raid under wraps until the situation was fully understood.

The Situation Room's Role in the Aftermath

As the news of bin Laden's death was confirmed, the Situation Room continued to play a key role in the operation's aftermath. The National Security Council and other high-level officials worked together to devise a strategy for dealing with the consequences of the mission.

The operation was a resounding success, but the risks involved were immense. In the end, the successful mission proved to be a turning point in the War on Terror and in the global fight against terrorism. It marked a significant victory for U.S. intelligence, military, and political coordination, as the operation was carried out with precision and professionalism.

In the months that followed, President Obama and his national security team would be faced with the diplomatic challenges of explaining the operation to the world, especially Pakistan, whose government was left in the dark about the raid. Despite the secrecy, the raid would go on to become one of the most defining moments of Obama's presidency, signaling the U.S.'s commitment to bringing terrorists to justice, no matter the cost.

The decision to launch the raid that killed Osama bin Laden was made in the White House Situation Room under immense pressure and uncertainty. Every moment leading up to the mission was filled with strategic discussions, intelligence assessments, and high-risk decisions. The successful operation, which resulted in the death of one of the most wanted terrorists in the world, was the result of years of intelligence work, careful planning, and real-time decisions. The Situation Room was the epicenter of the mission, where every decision counted, and the outcome would resonate for years to come.

CHAPTER 7

January 6th: The Capitol Under Siege

The storming of the U.S. Capitol on January 6, 2021, was one of the most shocking and significant events in recent American history. As rioters breached the halls of Congress, the nation watched in disbelief. Yet behind the scenes, in the White House Situation Room, a rapidly escalating crisis unfolded. This chapter takes a close look at the decisions, challenges, and actions taken within the Situation Room as the Capitol was under siege, focusing on the real-time responses from President Donald Trump, his advisers, and key officials who worked tirelessly to manage the volatile situation.

The Unfolding Crisis

On the morning of January 6, a joint session of Congress was convened to certify the Electoral College results, confirming Joe Biden's victory in the 2020 Presidential Election. As a large crowd of Trump supporters gathered in Washington, D.C., many of them gathered to listen to a speech given by the president, who had falsely claimed that the election had been stolen. After the rally, thousands of protestors marched toward the Capitol building, where the certification process was already underway.

Around 1:00 p.m. EST, as the rioters overwhelmed law enforcement, the Situation Room sprang into action. The president was made aware of the escalating violence, and security forces struggled to maintain control as rioters breached the Capitol grounds and entered the building. In real time, the Situation Room became the nerve center for coordinating the federal response to the violent assault on one of the most sacred symbols of American democracy.

The Situation Room's Initial Response

As the Capitol was under siege, decisions had to be made quickly. In the Situation Room, key personnel, including President Trump, Vice President Mike Pence, and senior advisers, were continuously briefed on the developing situation. Law enforcement and the National Guard, who had been previously prepared for crowd control, were now facing a significantly more violent and organized threat.

Early on, the response from President Trump was controversial. While his team in the Situation Room sought to coordinate federal resources to quell the violence, Trump was slow to call for immediate action. His advisers were pressing for a stronger response, but there was a key delay in fully mobilizing the National Guard and other law enforcement resources. The debate about how to respond, who should take charge, and what actions should be taken created tension in the room.

The Pressure Mounts: The Decision to Deploy the National Guard

As rioters stormed through the halls of the Capitol, lawmakers were forced to evacuate and hide in secure locations. The situation had quickly escalated from a protest to an insurrection. The urgent need for military support became clear, and the National Guard was activated, but the delays in the response raised questions about the chain of command and how prepared the Situation Room had been for such an event.

The decision to deploy the National Guard was not immediate. Despite the mounting threat, it took over 90 minutes for the deployment to be fully authorized. The delay was partly due to disagreements over whether the District of Columbia National Guard should be activated and who would ultimately be in command. D.C. National Guard officials were awaiting approval from the Secretary of Defense, who was receiving direction from the White House. In those critical moments, the Situation Room was filled with a sense of urgency, but also uncertainty about the proper course of action. The complexities of jurisdiction, command structure, and the sheer scale of the event created hurdles in mobilizing the necessary resources quickly.

Meanwhile, key advisers, including then-Chief of Staff Mark Meadows, were in constant communication with law enforcement agencies, military personnel, and local officials in D.C. They coordinated efforts to ensure that additional law enforcement units from outside the region could support local forces. At the same time, the FBI was monitoring intelligence sources to identify any potential threats from organized groups within the mob.

Trump's Response and the Role of Social Media

President Trump's initial response to the crisis was a subject of intense scrutiny. While the Situation Room was focused on securing the Capitol and ensuring safety, the president's public statements were under intense pressure. Trump posted a video message to the rioters, asking them to "go home," but at the same time, he reiterated his baseless claims of election fraud. The message failed to adequately condemn the violence, and his words were seen by many as a tacit endorsement of the rioters' actions.

This inaction fueled the crisis further, as the president's refusal to fully denounce the violence and issue stronger calls for dispersal prolonged the chaos. His social media presence, especially on Twitter, played a significant role in shaping the response. Trump's words continued to spark defiance among the rioters and emboldened them, delaying any de-escalation.

Inside the Situation Room, senior advisers and officials struggled with the implications of the president's stance. They were pushing for a more forceful and unequivocal response, but the president's public messages did not align with the severity of the situation. As Trump continued to voice support for the rioters, pressure mounted for him to take more decisive action.

The Role of Law Enforcement and Military Coordination

As the Capitol Police were overwhelmed, law enforcement agencies from across the country were mobilized to assist. The FBI, ATF, and other agencies were activated, but it was the arrival of the National Guard that would eventually make the difference. After hours of negotiation, the National Guard units were deployed to provide crucial support. By the time the Guard arrived at the Capitol, the rioters had already caused significant damage, and the building was in disarray. However, the additional law enforcement presence helped to push back the mob and regain control of the Capitol.

Throughout this time, the Situation Room was in constant communication with military leaders, law enforcement, and local officials. Real-time intelligence was being relayed to the White House as the rioters continued to rampage through the Capitol. Each decision made in the Situation Room had immediate consequences on the ground, with advisers working to coordinate federal assistance to restore order.

A Nation in Crisis: The Aftermath

Once the Capitol was cleared and the rioters dispersed, the full scope of the event became clear. Five people lost their lives in the violence, and the damage to the Capitol was extensive. The insurrection had left the country grappling with the very real consequences of an attack on democracy itself.

The Situation Room, which had been on high alert during the event, continued to play a critical role as the nation began to assess the damage. President Trump, under pressure from political leaders on both sides of the aisle, finally issued a stronger condemnation of the violence. His response, though, was seen by many as insufficient for the scale of the crisis. The event raised questions about how much responsibility the president bore for inciting the mob and for failing to act quickly enough to quell the violence.

The January 6th Capitol riot remains a defining moment in American political history. The actions—or lack thereof—inside the Situation Room that day have had lasting consequences, both for national security protocols and for the political landscape. As the country recovered from the shock of the riot, questions about leadership, accountability, and the future of U.S. democracy continued to linger.

The Capitol riot of January 6, 2021, revealed the vulnerabilities in the U.S. political system and the challenges that emerge when national security is threatened. Inside the Situation Room, the response to the crisis was shaped by a combination of strategic decisions, bureaucratic delays, and political considerations. The tensions between presidential leadership, law enforcement coordination, and the urgency of the moment proved to be a delicate balance that ultimately played out in full view of the nation.

Conclusion

The White House Situation Room has been the crucible of decision-making during some of the most critical moments in American history. From the assassination attempts on Presidents Kennedy and Reagan to the 9/11 attacks and the mission that killed Osama Bin Laden, it has been the place where the fate of the nation was often decided in real time. The decisions made within those walls have shaped U.S. history, influenced global events, and helped define the course of presidential leadership in moments of crisis. As we reflect on these high-stakes situations, it's clear that the Situation Room's role in crisis management will continue to evolve, guiding future leaders through the complexities of modern geopolitics and national security.

Shaping U.S. History and Global Affairs

Throughout the decades, the decisions made in the Situation Room have had profound consequences, not only on the immediate outcomes of crises but also on U.S. foreign policy and the country's standing on the world stage. In 1961, President Kennedy's creation of the Situation Room was a direct response to the chaos of the Bay of Pigs invasion, a failure that underscored the need for centralized, real-time communication and decision-making. The room became a symbol of U.S. leadership under pressure, a space where the most critical choices would unfold—choices that would ripple across the globe. The Cuban Missile Crisis, for example, saw Kennedy and his advisers grapple with the prospect of nuclear war, balancing military and diplomatic solutions under the direst of circumstances. The decisions made there not only preserved American security but also altered the dynamics of Cold War politics.

Fast forward to the 21st century, and the Situation Room was again at the center of monumental events. On September 11, 2001, as terrorist attacks unfolded across the country, the Situation Room became the command center for a rapid and coordinated response. Decisions made in those early hours set the course for the War on Terror, the reshaping of U.S. defense policies, and the international fight against al-Qaeda. Similarly, in the months leading up to the successful raid that killed Osama Bin Laden in 2011, the Situation Room witnessed a high-stakes, precision-driven decision-making process. The operation not only marked a pivotal moment in the fight against terrorism but also showcased the importance of intelligence, military cooperation, and rapid decision-making in achieving national security objectives.

In each of these cases, the Situation Room served as a crucial mechanism for maintaining order and ensuring that the president and his team were equipped with the information and support necessary to act swiftly and decisively. The outcomes of these events, shaped by those moments of crisis management, influenced not just American policy but global geopolitics, from international alliances to the balance of power in the Middle East and beyond.

Lessons Learned from Crisis Management

The Situation Room's legacy is not just one of decisive actions but also one of lessons learned. As each crisis unfolded, both successes and failures became integral in shaping future decision-making frameworks. The 9/11 attacks highlighted the need for faster and more efficient information-sharing, coordination between agencies, and the development of systems that could quickly respond to evolving threats. The attacks exposed gaps in intelligence, gaps that were later addressed through improved communication technologies and the establishment of more robust frameworks for interagency collaboration. These lessons were vital in the years that followed, as the U.S. responded to an ever-shifting landscape of security challenges, from cyberattacks to foreign espionage and geopolitical instability.

Similarly, the botched rescue mission during the Iran Hostage Crisis in 1980 underscored the importance of preparation and contingency planning. The failure of Operation Eagle Claw, which was supposed to free American hostages in Tehran, was a sobering reminder of how a lack of coordination and failure to account for unexpected variables could jeopardize national security. The lessons from that operation reshaped military strategies, led to the creation of more specialized task forces, and redefined the U.S. approach to international hostage situations. This, in turn, influenced decisions in the years to come, such as the successful raid that killed Bin Laden, where planning, intelligence, and the ability to react to unforeseen challenges were key to success.

The decision-making that unfolded in the Situation Room during these crises also revealed the complexities of leadership under pressure. The presidents involved had to balance competing interests—political, military, and public opinion—while making decisions that would impact the lives of Americans and people around the world. Their ability to make decisions quickly, often without all the facts, and to maintain the confidence of the American people in the face of uncertainty, has become an integral part of presidential crisis management.

Evolving Technology and Security Measures
The role of technology in the Situation Room has transformed dramatically since its inception. When President Kennedy created the room in

the early 1960s, the communication tools at his disposal were relatively rudimentary compared to the technological advancements of today. In those early days, the Situation Room relied on secure telephones, maps, and manual communication methods. Today, it is equipped with state-of-the-art technology, including real-time satellite feeds, video conferencing, and sophisticated data analytics systems. This evolution has made it possible for decision-makers to receive instant updates from anywhere in the world, enabling a quicker, more informed response to crises.

The integration of modern technology has also made it easier for the Situation Room to coordinate with intelligence agencies, military commands, and international allies in real-time. During the Bin Laden raid, for example, live feeds from drones and surveillance teams were transmitted to the Situation Room, providing President Obama and his advisers with a continuous stream of information as the mission unfolded. This level of real-time intelligence gathering and coordination would have been unimaginable just a few decades ago, and it represents the growing role that technology plays in shaping the decisions made in these high-pressure environments.

In addition to technological advancements, the Situation Room has also seen improvements in the security measures surrounding presidential decision-making. The rise of cyber threats, international hacking attempts, and the growing sophistication of adversaries have made the need for enhanced cybersecurity more critical than ever. As a result, the Situation Room is equipped with some of the most secure systems to protect sensitive information and ensure that national security is never compromised.

The Future of Crisis Decision-Making

As the world becomes increasingly interconnected and complex, the Situation Room will continue to evolve as the heart of presidential decision-making during times of crisis. The future will likely bring new challenges, from emerging cyber threats to the changing dynamics of global power. As technology continues to advance, the tools available in the Situation Room will become even more sophisticated, allowing for quicker decision-making, better coordination, and more effective responses to global challenges.

The lessons learned from past crises will undoubtedly shape how future presidents approach crisis management. The ability to make informed, decisive decisions under pressure will remain at the core of U.S. leadership, whether in dealing with a natural disaster, a terrorist attack, or a diplomatic standoff. The Situation Room will continue to be a symbol of presidential authority and responsibility, a place where the fate of the nation and the world can hinge on the choices made in those high-stakes moments.

The Situation Room has proven time and again to be an essential component of American presidential decision-making. Its role in shaping U.S. history—through its involvement in events like the Cuban Missile Crisis, 9/11, and the Bin Laden raid—has left an indelible mark on the nation's security, policies, and global standing. As crises continue to evolve and become more complex, the Situation Room will remain a critical space for the nation's leaders to make choices that define the course of history. The lessons learned from past crises will continue to guide presidential decision-making, ensuring that the U.S. remains ready to meet the challenges of the future, no matter how daunting they may be.

Acknowledgments

This book is the result of countless hours of research, writing, and collaboration, and it would not have been possible without the support and contributions of many individuals.

To the researchers, historians, and journalists who have meticulously documented the pivotal events explored in these pages, your work laid the foundation for this book. To my editor, whose sharp eye and thoughtful guidance brought clarity and focus to the narrative, thank you for helping shape this story. To my friends and family, your unwavering encouragement provided the fuel I needed to see this project through to completion.

A special acknowledgment to those who have served in public office and national security roles, many of whom provided invaluable insights into the workings of the White House Situation Room. Your dedication and commitment to serving the nation continue to inspire.

Lastly, to the readers, thank you for joining me on this journey through some of the most critical moments in American history. It is for you that this book was written—to bring light to the hidden stories and decisions that have shaped our world.

Note from the Author

The stories in this book are not just about decisions; they are about the people who made them, the challenges they faced, and the profound impacts those moments have had on the course of history. My aim is to bring you as close as possible to the heartbeat of these events, sharing insights into how leadership operates under unimaginable pressure.

As you turn these pages, I hope you gain a deeper understanding of the complexity of decision-making at the highest levels and a greater appreciation for the responsibility borne by those in positions of power.

Thank you for allowing me to share these stories with you. It is my hope that they resonate, inform, and spark meaningful conversations about leadership, resilience, and the role of history in shaping our shared future.